GRANDER

EARLY READING ACADEMY

Volume

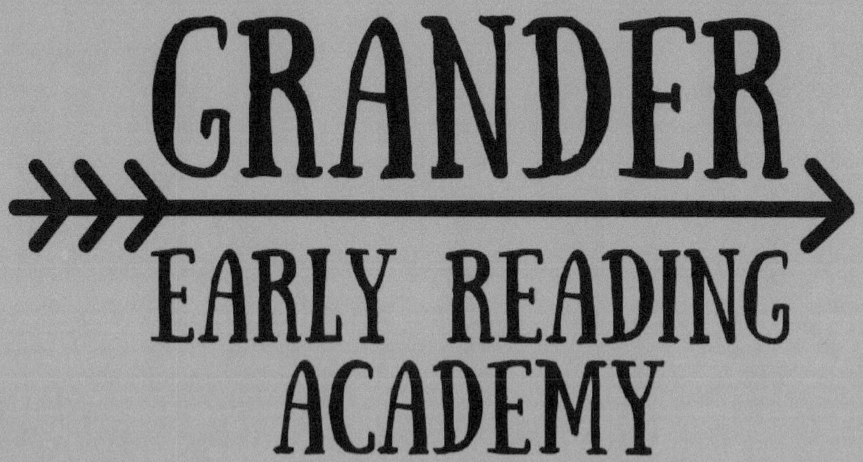
GRANDER
EARLY READING
ACADEMY

Grander
PUBLISHING

GRANDER

EARLY READING ACADEMY

Volume

ONE

FEATURING

THIS IS THE FIRST DAY OF SCHOOL
&
WE SAW THE BEARS

WE SAW
THE BEARS

I saw bears run by the hill.

The big bear went up the hill.

The little bear went down the hill.

I saw the brown bear eat a fish.

I saw the white bear eat a fish.

I saw the black bear eat a fish.

All the bears like to eat fish.

My father saw the bears too.

He said he could sit and
look at them all day.

We had to go home.
ZOO
Thank You for Visiting
LGM ZAM

That was a good day!

I want to see more bears.

Comprehension Questions

1. Which bear went up the hill?

2. Which bear went down the hill?

3. What are the colors of the bears?

4. What did the bears eat?

Answers

1. The big bear
2. The little bear

3. Brown, Black, White
4. Fish

Common Sight Words

saw	eat
by	see
hill	he
bear	the
fish	all
sit	up

THIS IS
THE FIRST DAY
OF SCHOOL

This is the first day of school.

I will go to school on the big yellow bus.

I will write.

My teacher will be so kind.

She will help me.

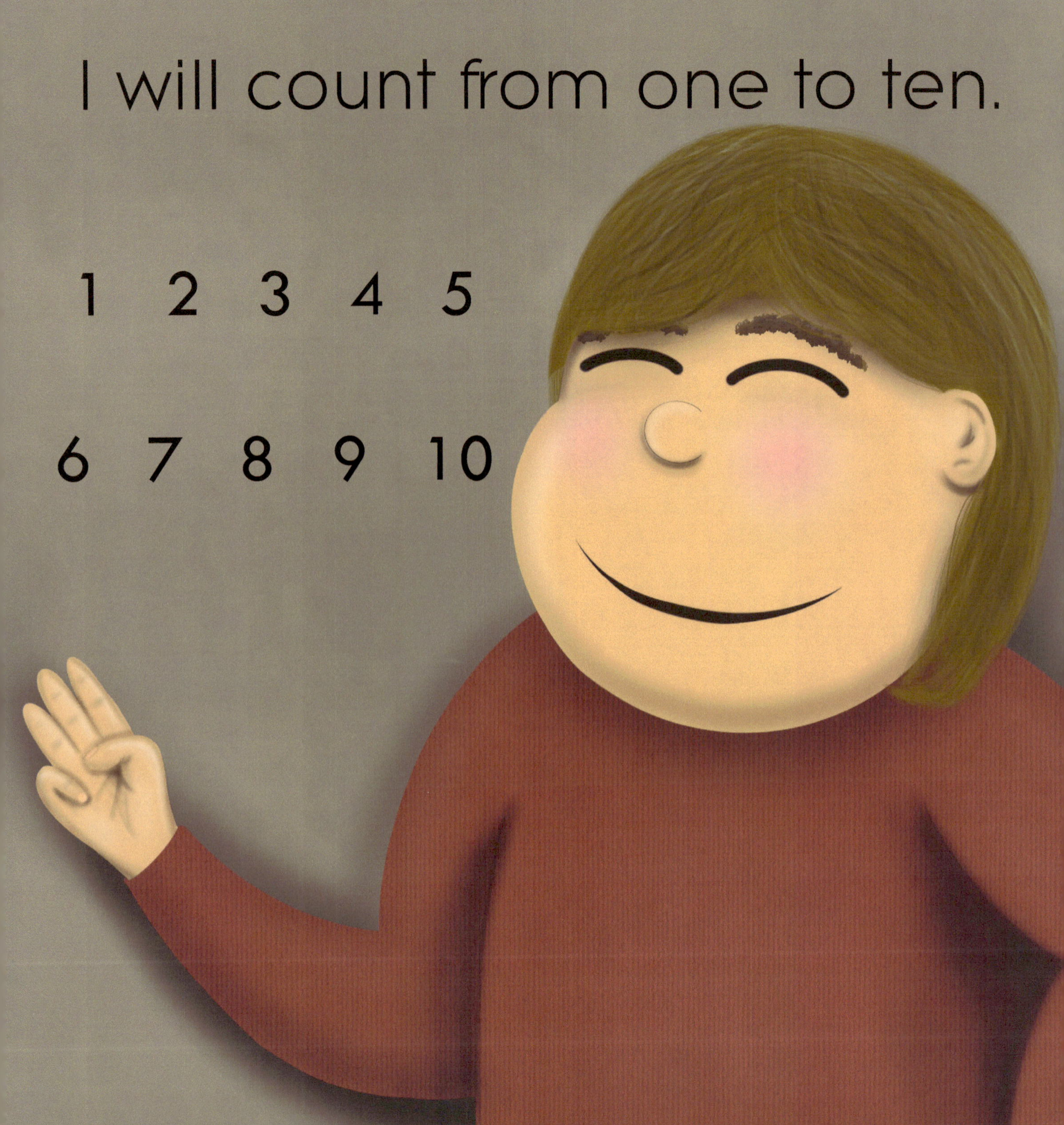
I will count from one to ten.
1 2 3 4 5
6 7 8 9 10

I will draw.

I will sit and eat.
MILK
MOO
2%

I will run and jump when
we go out to play.

Ben and Jen
will be there.

They will run
and jump too.

I will like school.
It will be so fun!

SCHOOL

<u>Comprehension Questions</u>

1. What color is the bus?

2. What are 3 things that the kid will do at school before they go out to play?

3. Who will be there when they go out to play?

4. What 2 things will they do when they go out to play?

<u>Answers</u>

1. Yellow

2. Draw, Write, Count, Sit and Eat

3. Ben and Jen

4. Run and Jump

Common Sight Words

will	sit
day	go
and	big
run	be
fun	one
bus	ten

Thank you so much
teachers and all
school personel for
your dedication
to our youth.

Thank you parents and
grandparents for
reading to your
children and
grandchildren.

YOU MAKE A DIFFERENCE!

www.ingramcontent.com/pod-product-compliance
Lightning Source LLC
Chambersburg PA
CBHW042011110726
48006CB00004B/1040